UNBELIEVABLE!

34 AMAZING FACTS ABOUT BASKETBALL

Matt Doeden

Lerner Publications ◆ Minneapolis

Lerner Publications Company
An imprint of Lerner Publishing Group, Inc.
241 First Avenue North
Minneapolis, MN 55401 USA

For reading levels and more information, look up this title at www.lernerbooks.com.

Main body text set in ITC Franklin Gothic Std.
Typeface provided by Adobe Systems.

Designer: Mary Ross
Lerner team: Sue Marquis

Library of Congress Cataloging-in-Publication Data

Names: Doeden, Matt, author.
Title: 34 amazing facts about basketball / Matt Doeden.
Other titles: Thirty-four amazing facts about basketball
Description: Minneapolis, MN : Lerner Publications, [2024] | Series: UpDog books.
   Unbelievable! | Includes bibliographical references and index. | Audience: Ages
   8–11 years | Audience: Grades 2–3 | Summary: "Discover incredible facts
   about basketball, one of the world's most popular sports. The game's amazing
   moments, biggest wins, and most outrageous plays are all here in a fun, high-
   interest format"— Provided by publisher.
Identifiers: LCCN 2023010091 (print) | LCCN 2023010092
   (ebook) | ISBN 9798765608982 (lib. bdg.) | ISBN 9798765625118 (pbk.) |
   ISBN 9798765618783 (epub)
Subjects: LCSH: Basketball—Miscellanea—Juvenile literature. | BISAC: JUVENILE
   NONFICTION / Sports & Recreation / Basketball
Classification: LCC GV885.1 .D627 2024 (print) | LCC GV885.1 (ebook) |
   DDC 796.323—dc23/eng/20230308

LC record available at https://lccn.loc.gov/2023010091
LC ebook record available at https://lccn.loc.gov/2023010092

Manufactured in the United States of America
1-1009230-51576-4/26/2023

Table of Contents

THE CHANGING GAME

The first basketball game was in 1891. The baskets were peach baskets.

Basketball inventor James Naismith

Players used ladders to get basketballs out of the baskets.

The first women's
college game
was in 1896.

Stanford beat California, Berkeley, 2–1.

In the 1930s, players began using jump shots.

In 1979, the National Basketball Association (NBA) added the three-point line.

Up Next!

THRILLING RECORDS.

GREAT MOMENTS

Wilt Chamberlain's size and skill made him great.

Wilt Chamberlain

In 1962, he set an NBA record
with 100 points in one game.

The Women's National Basketball Association (WNBA) started in 1997.

In 2002, Lisa Leslie made
the league's first slam dunk.

Stephen Curry is the NBA's best shooter.

In the 2015–2016 season, he set a record with 402 three-point baskets.

Who are pro basketball's highest scorers? Here are the top five in the NBA and the WNBA!

NBA player	Career points
1. LeBron James	38,652
2. Kareem Abdul-Jabbar	38,387
3. Karl Malone	36,928
4. Kobe Bryant	33,643
5. Michael Jordan	32,292

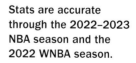

LeBron James

Stats are accurate through the 2022–2023 NBA season and the 2022 WNBA season.

Diana Taurasi

WNBA player	Career points
1. Diana Taurasi	9,693
2. Tina Thompson	7,488
3. Tamika Catchings	7,380
4. Tina Charles	7,115
5. Candice Dupree	6,895

Up Next!

TEAMWORK.

TEAM SPORT

The Boston Celtics were a dynasty in the 1950s and 1960s.

They won 11 championships in 13 years.

The Celtics have won 17 total NBA championships.

They are tied with the Los Angeles Lakers for the most in the league.

Los Angeles Lakers players celebrate.

The Connecticut women's basketball team has 11 college championships.

They had back-to-back unbeaten seasons in 2008–2009 and 2009–2010.

The 2009–2010 Connecticut Huskies

Up Next!

WILD AND AWESOME.

AMAZING BUT TRUE

In 1983, the Detroit Pistons beat the Denver Nuggets 186–184.

It was the highest-scoring game in NBA history.

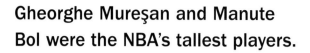

Gheorghe Mureşan and Manute Bol were the NBA's tallest players.

Gheorghe Mureşan

Manute Bol

At 7 feet 7 (2.3 m), they towered over others.

The WNBA designed their balls to stand out.

The league was the first to use orange-and-oatmeal basketballs.

Glossary

dynasty: a team that is successful for a long time

jump shot: when a player jumps and shoots before landing

slam dunk: a shot made by jumping and throwing the ball down through the basket

three-point line: a line on the court beyond which a shot counts for three points

unbeaten: having no losses all season

Check It Out!

Doeden, Matt. *G.O.A.T. Men's Basketball Teams*. Minneapolis: Lerner Publications, 2021.

Fishman, Jon M. *Tina Charles vs. Lisa Leslie: Who Would Win?* Minneapolis: Lerner Publications, 2024.

Flynn, Brendan. *The Genius Kid's Guide to Pro Basketball*. Mendota Heights, MN: North Star Kids, 2022.

Jr. NBA
https://jr.nba.com/

Sports Illustrated Kids: Basketball
https://www.sikids.com/basketball

WNBA
https://www.wnba.com/

Index

Photo Acknowledgments

Image credits: Pongnathee Kluaythong/EyeEm/Getty Images, p. 3;
agefotostock/Alamy, p. 4; Courtesy of Springfield College, Archives
and Special Collections, p. 5; FPG/Archive Photos/Getty Images, p. 6;
Kirn Vintage Stock/Corbis/Getty Images, p. 7; H. Armstrong Roberts/
ClassicStock/Getty Images, p. 8; Focus on Sport/Getty Images, pp. 9, 18,
26, 27; Bettmann/Getty Images, pp. 10, 11, 19, 24; Todd Warshaw/Getty
Images, p. 12; Lisa Blumenfeld/NBAE/Getty Images, p. 13; Stacy Revere/
Getty Images, p. 14; Kevin C. Cox/Getty Images, p. 15; Jason Armond/
Los Angeles Times/Getty Images, p. 16; Christian Petersen/Getty Images,
p. 17; Matthew West/MediaNews Group/Boston Herald/Getty Images,
p. 20; Douglas P. DeFelice/Getty Images, p. 21; Elsa/Getty Images, p. 22;
Jeff Gross/Getty Images, p. 23; Wongsaphat Suknachon/EyeEm/Getty
Images, p. 25; Chitose Suzuki/Las Vegas Review-Journal/Tribune News
Service/Getty Images, p. 28; Maddie Meyer/Getty Images, p. 29.

Cover: REUTERS/Adrees Latif SN/Alamy Stock Photo.